LEARN YOUR ABC'S THROUGH ART WITH ME

LEARN YOUR ABC'S THROUGH ART WITH ME

Author & Illustrator: Pettina Yelez

Learn your ABCs through art with me

Copyright © 2025 by Pettina Velez. All rights reserved.

No part of this publication may be reproduced, distributed, or transmitted in any form or by any means, including photocopying, recording, or other electronic or mechanical methods, without the prior written permission of the author, except in the case of brief quotations embodied in critical reviews and certain other noncommercial uses permitted by copyright law.

This is a work of fiction. Unless otherwise indicated, all the names, characters, businesses, places, events and incidents in this book are either the product of the author's imagination or used in a fictitious manner. Any resemblance to actual persons, living or dead, or actual events is purely coincidental.

Printed in the United States of America
ISBN 978-1-967279-35-7 (hc)
ISBN 978-1-967279-34-0 (sc)
ISBN 978-1-967279-36-4 (e)

05.14.2025

This book is printed on acid-free paper.

The contents of this work, including, but not limited to, the accuracy of events, people, and places depicted; opinions expressed; permission to use previously published materials included; and any advice given or actions advocated are solely the responsibility of the author, who assumes all liability for said work and indemnifies the publisher against any claims stemming from publication of the work.

Blue Ink Media Solutions
1111B S Governors Ave
STE 7582 Dover,
DE 19904

www.blueinkmediasolutions.com

Dedication

This book is dedicated to my Grandchildren and all the kids I have cared for throughout the years.

Last but not the least, my sissy poo, Sheryl, my favorite critic.

I love you all.

-Tee Tee

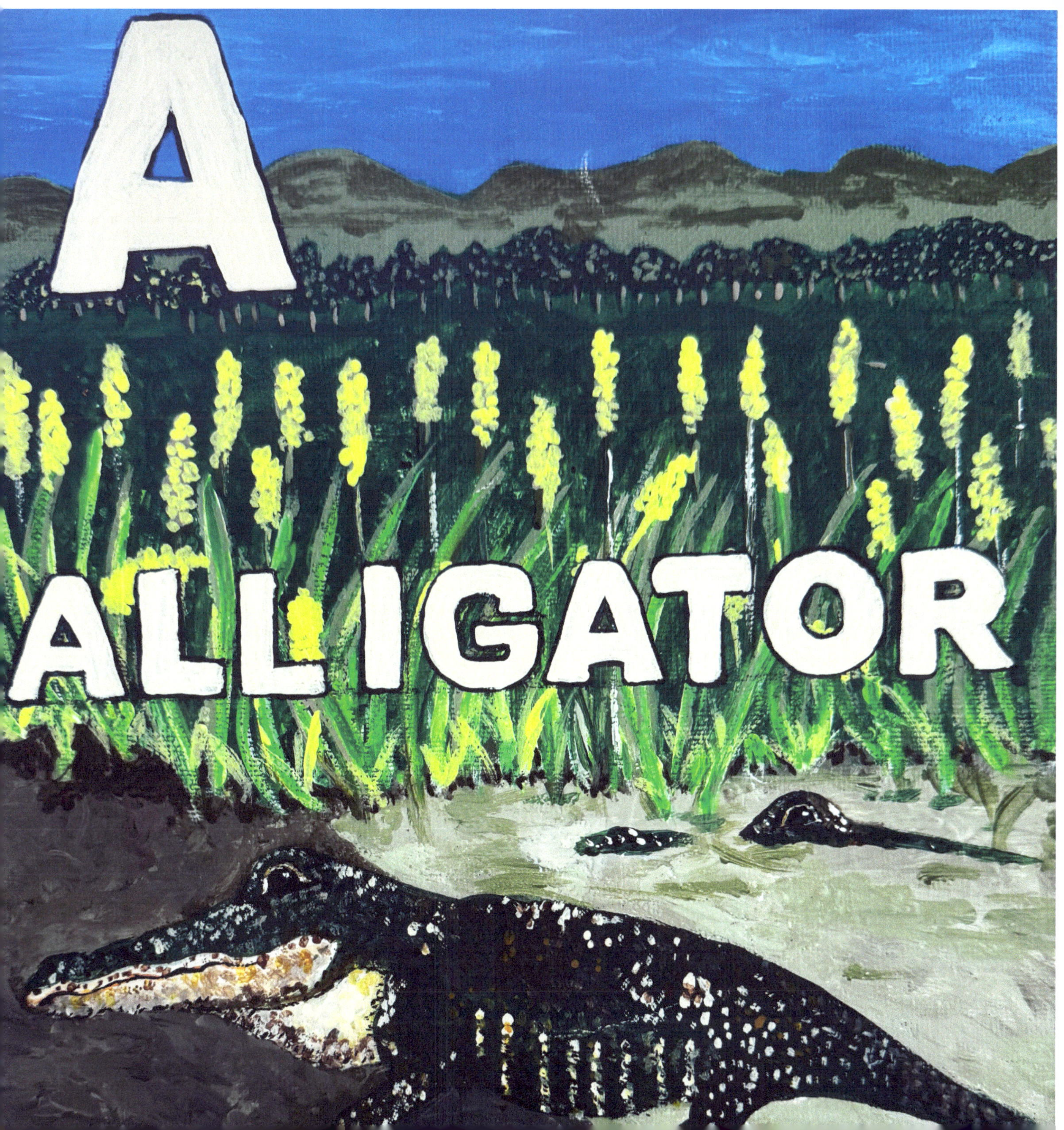

A
ALLIGATOR

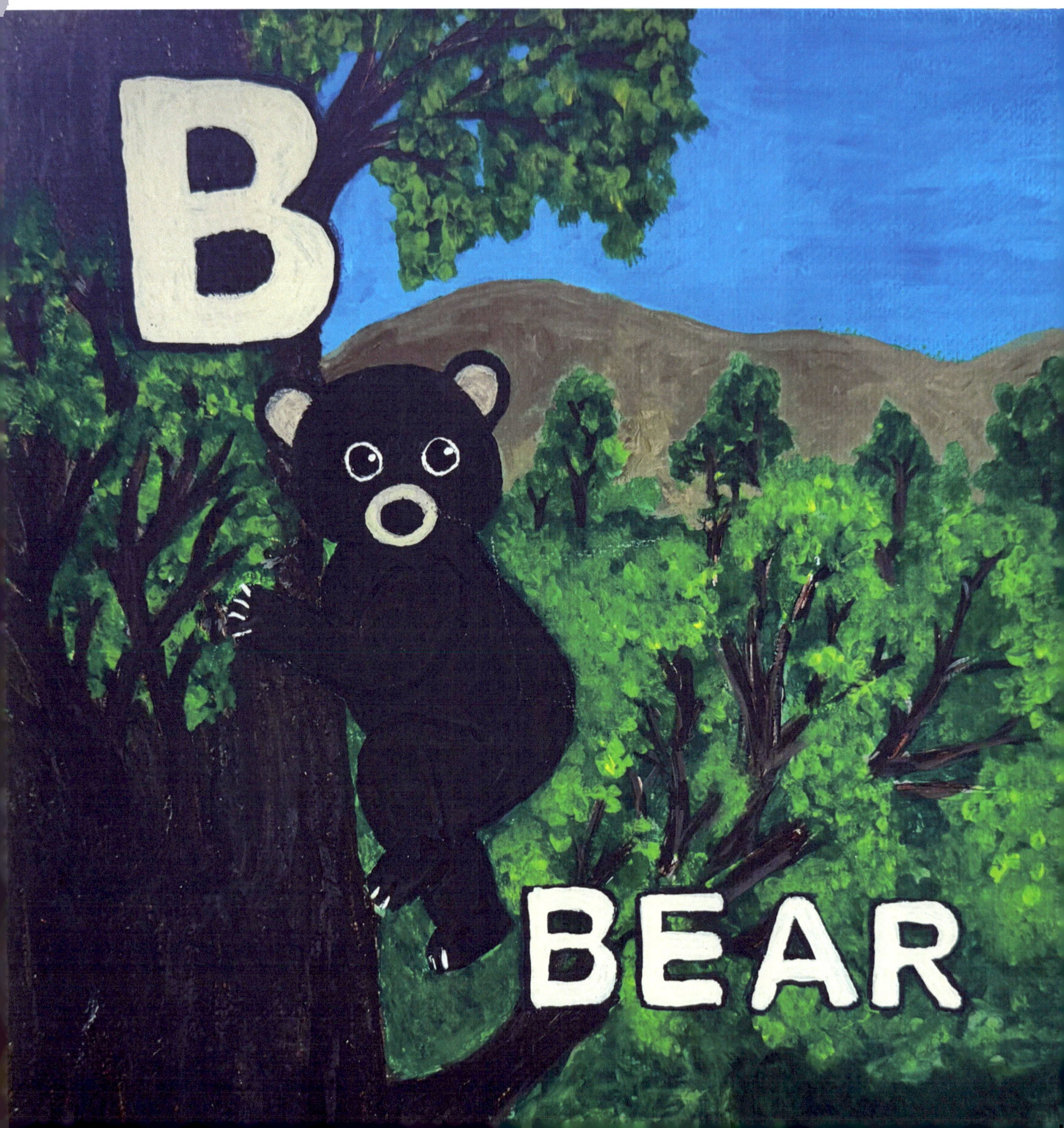

B

BEAR

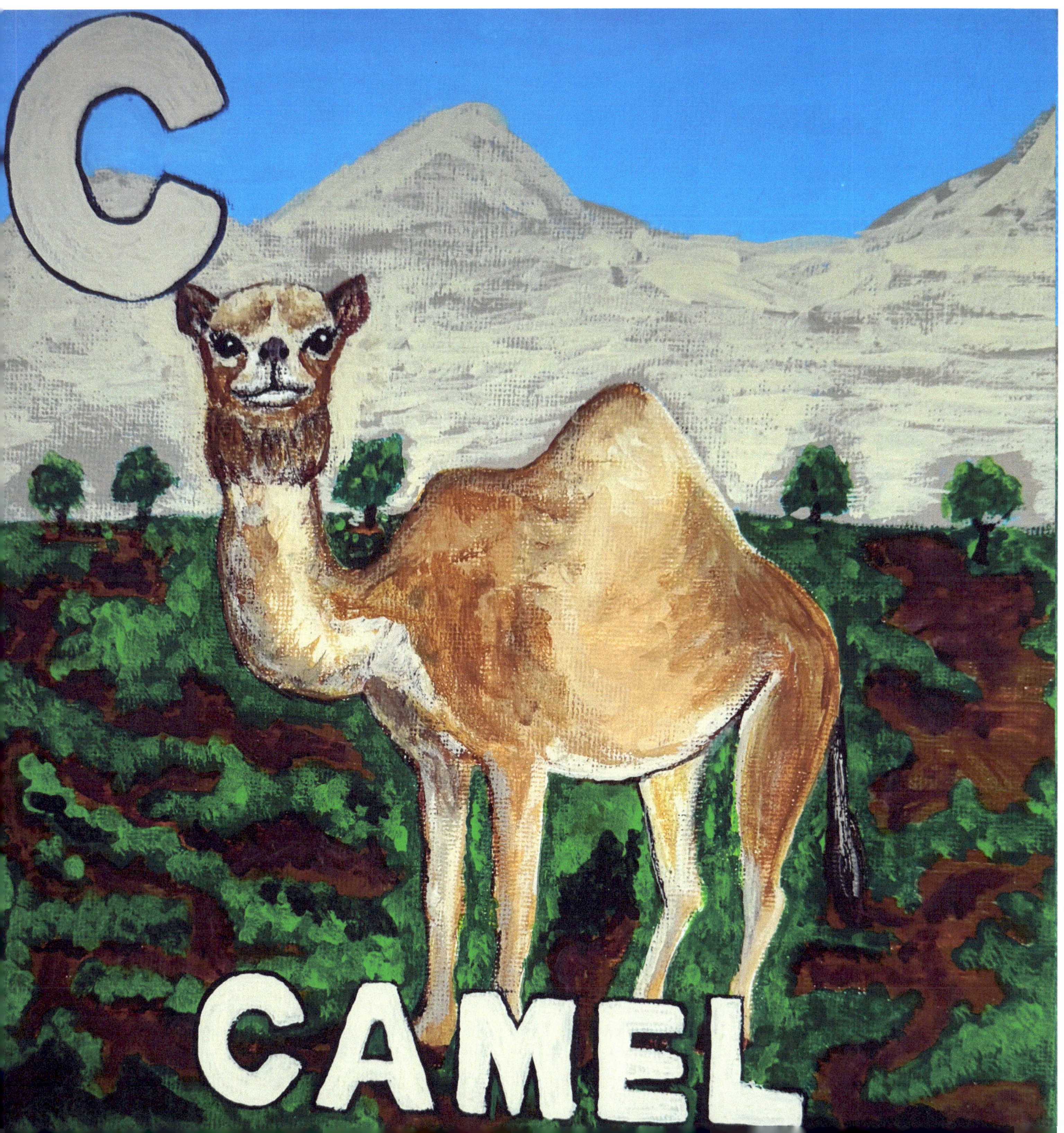

C
CAMEL

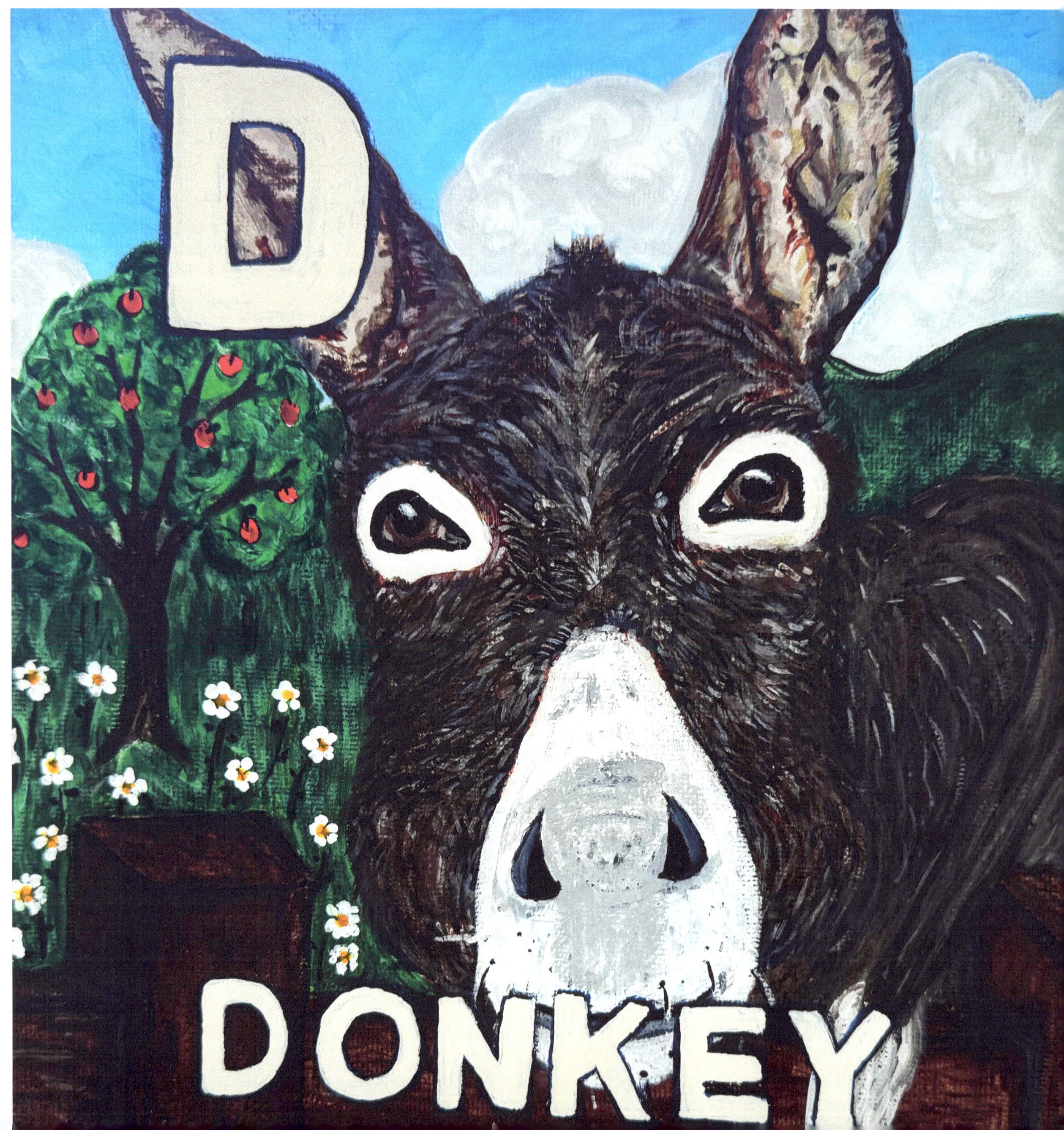

D
DONKEY

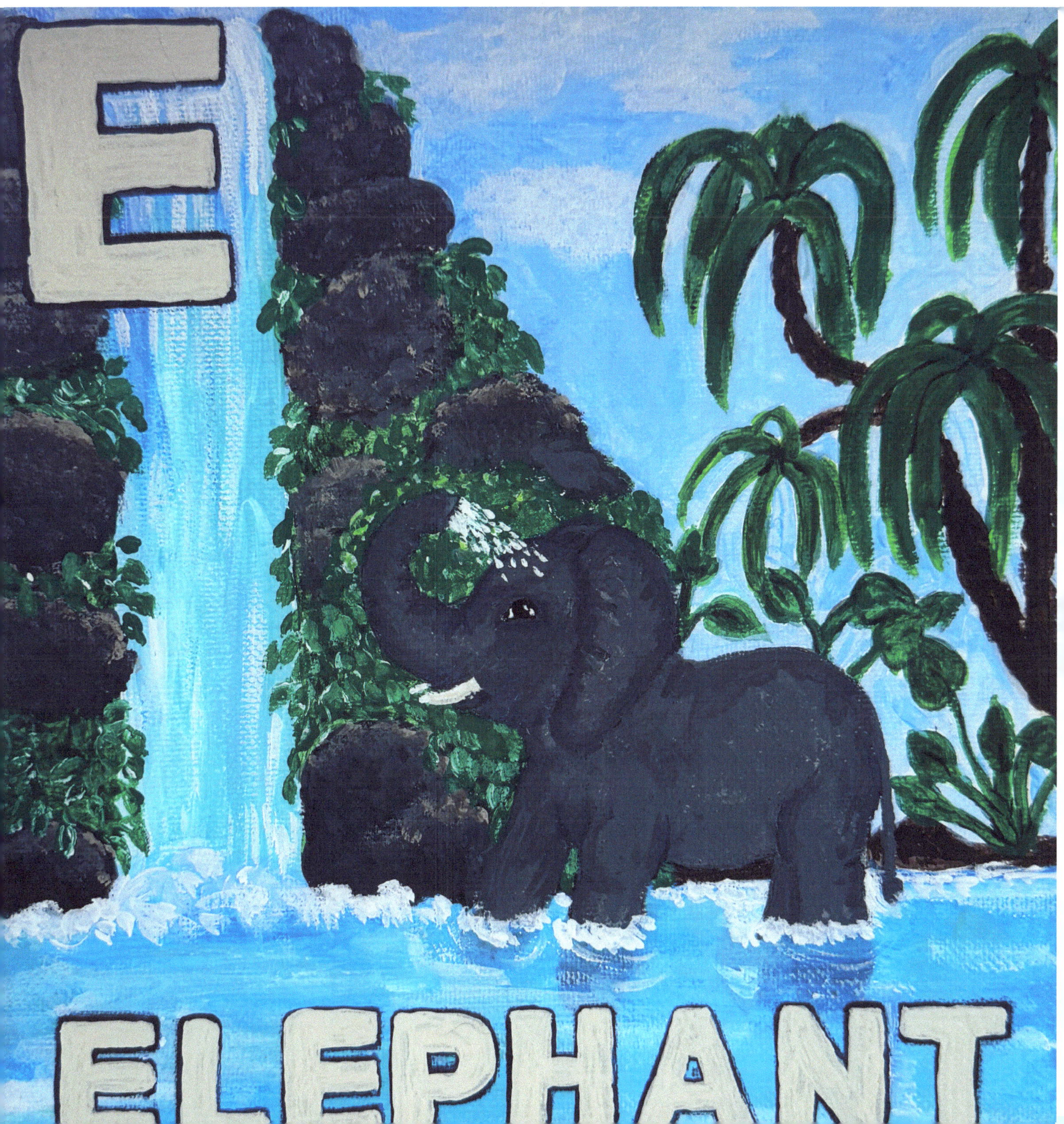

E
ELEPHANT

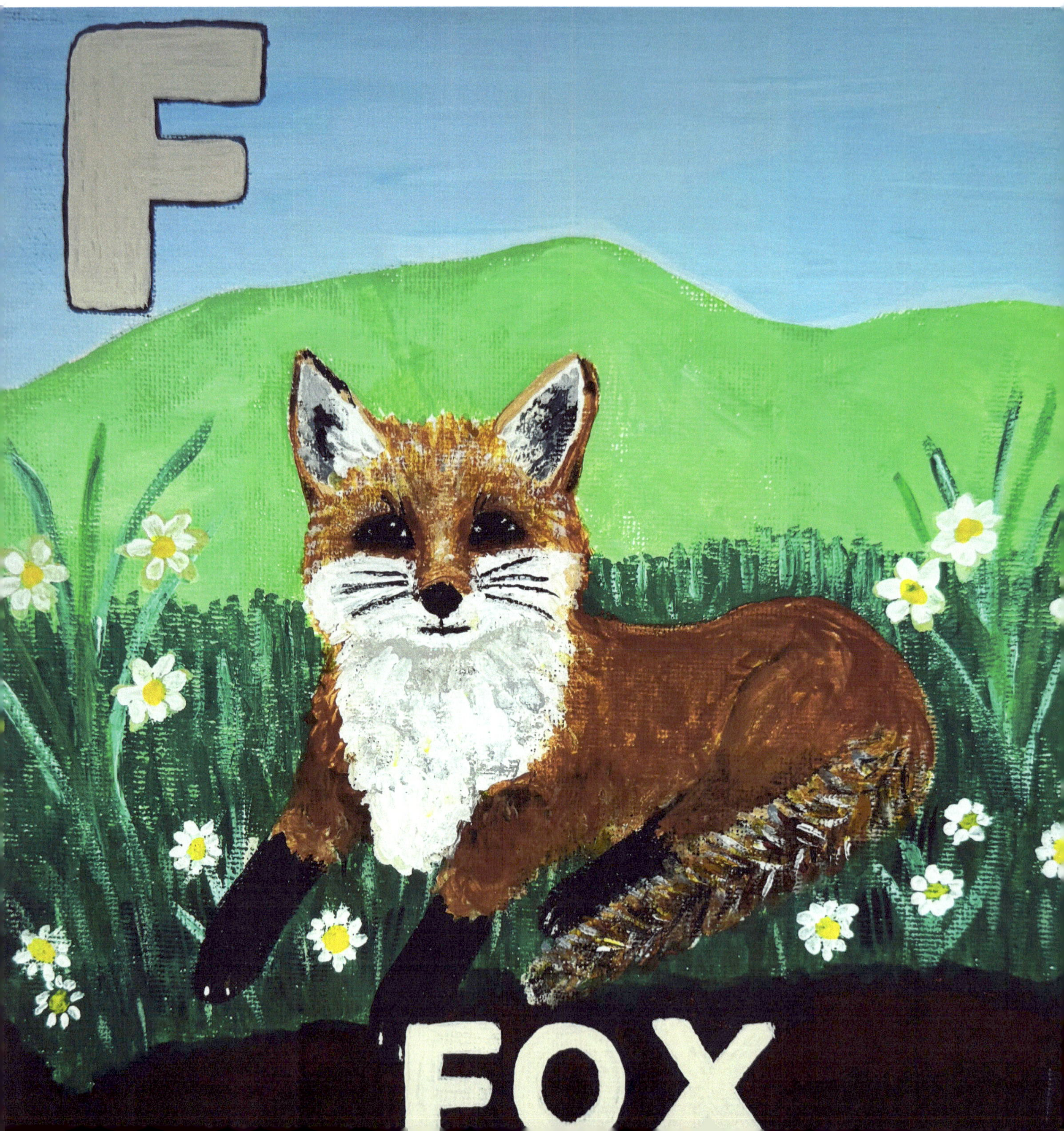
F
FOX

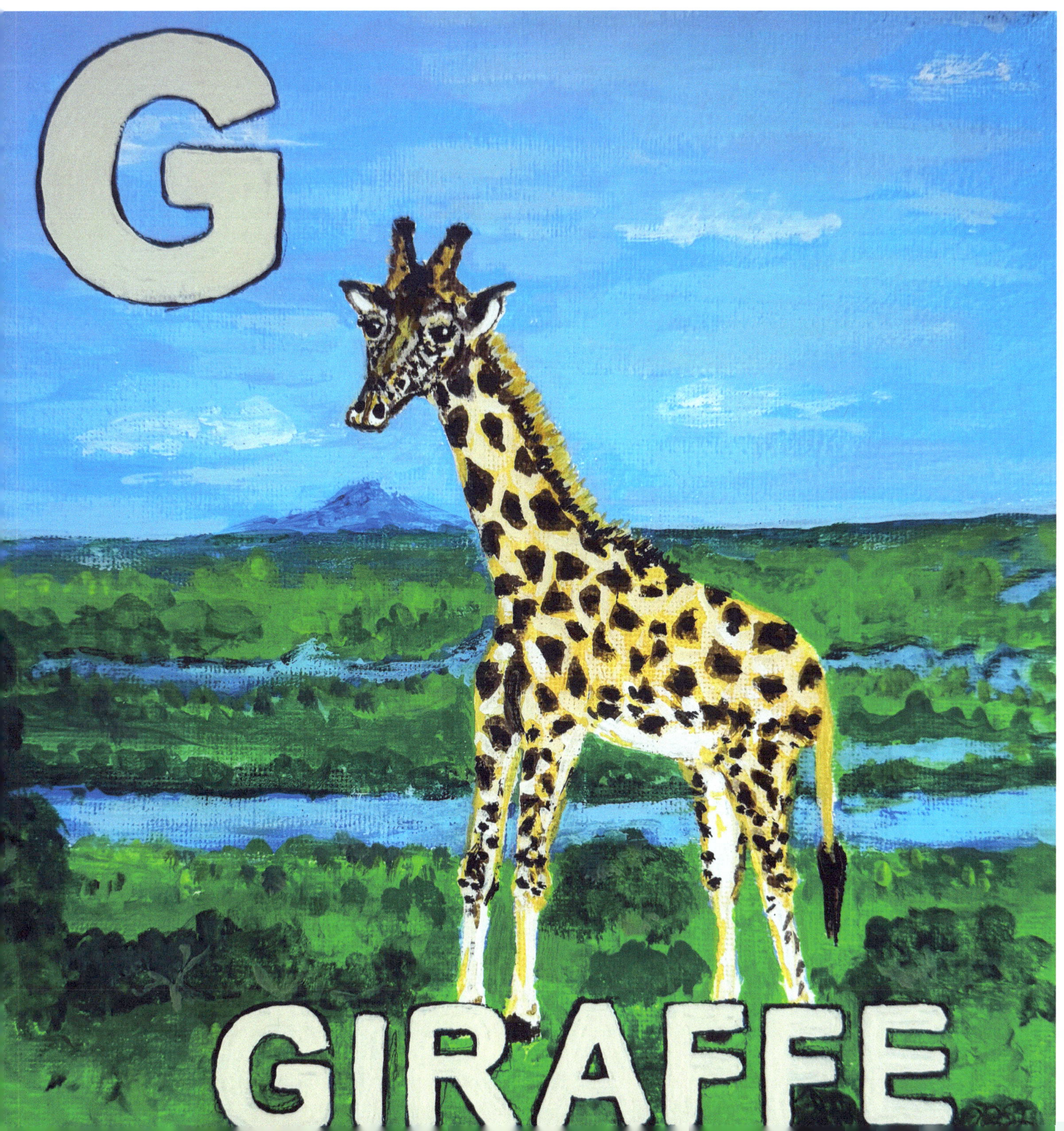

G
GIRAFFE

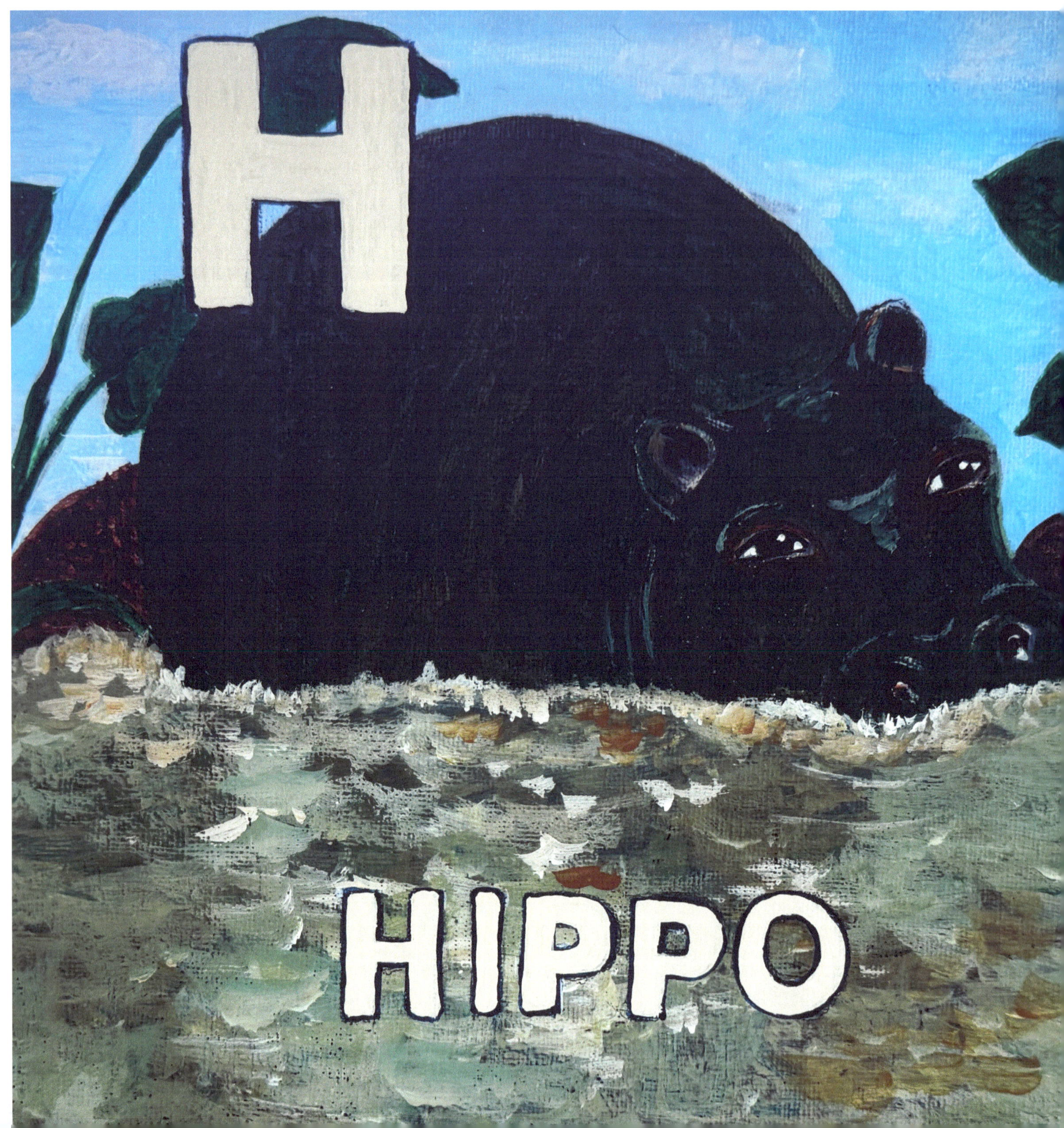
H
HIPPO

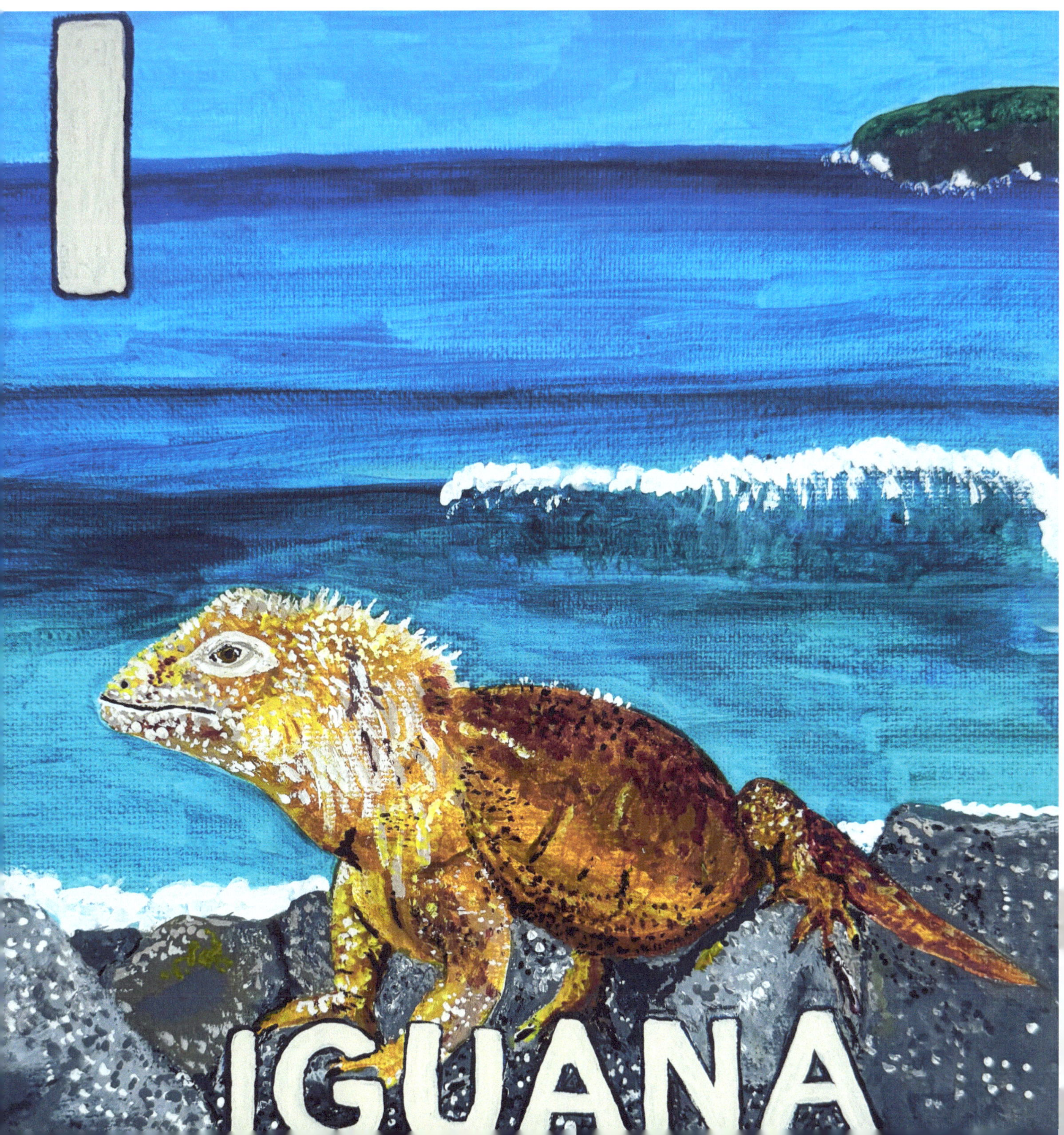

I
IGUANA

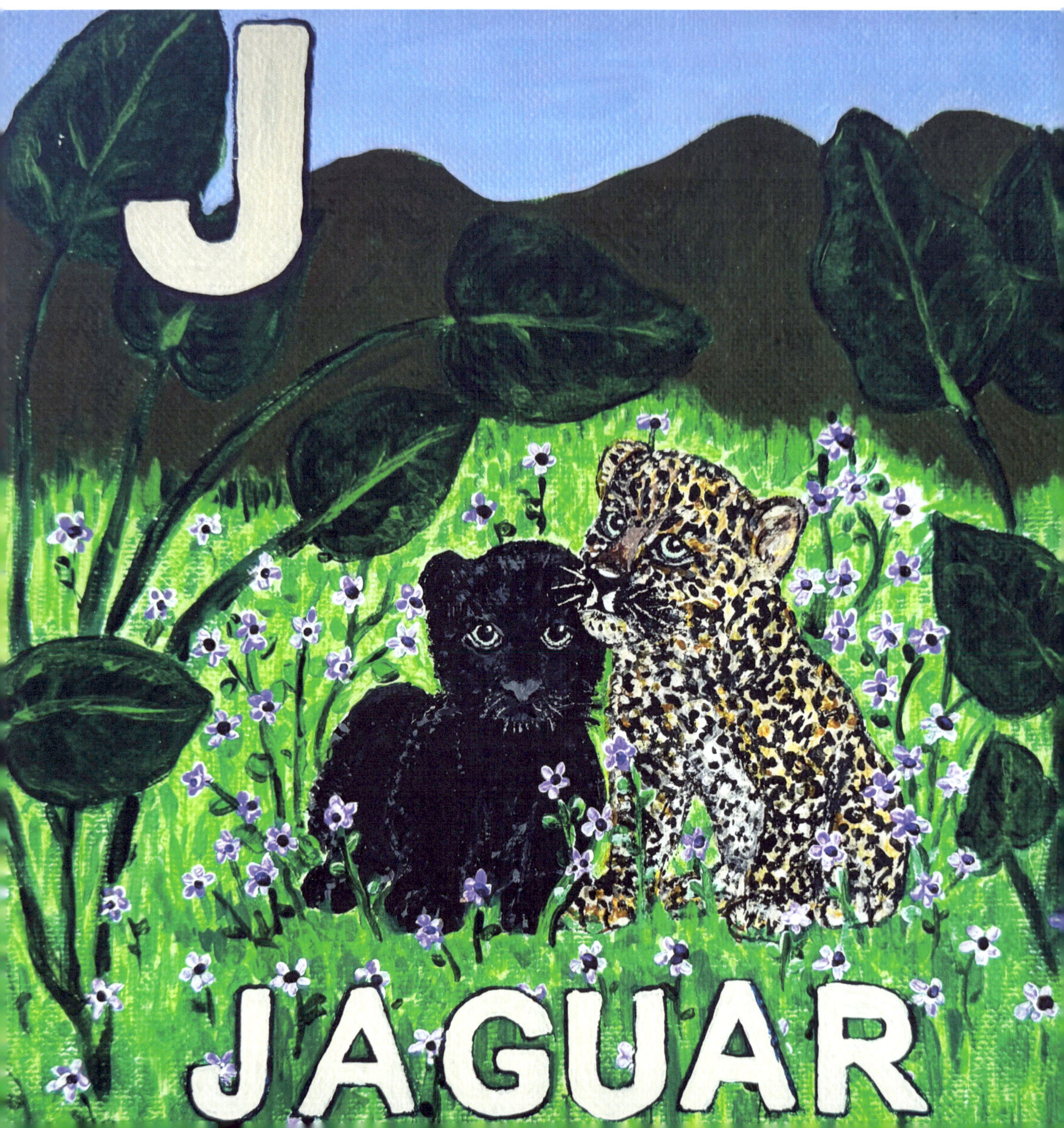

J
JAGUAR

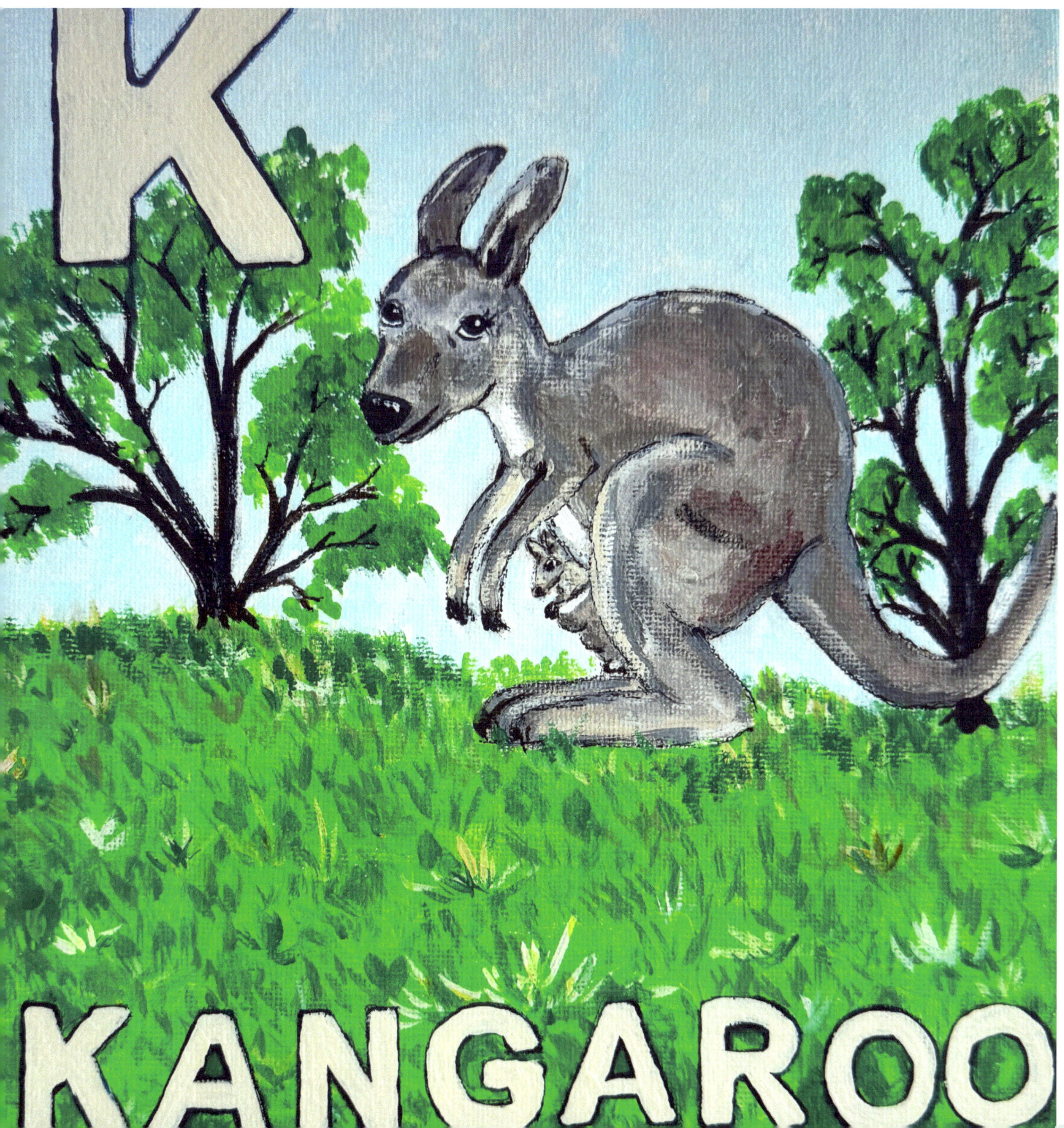

K
KANGAROO

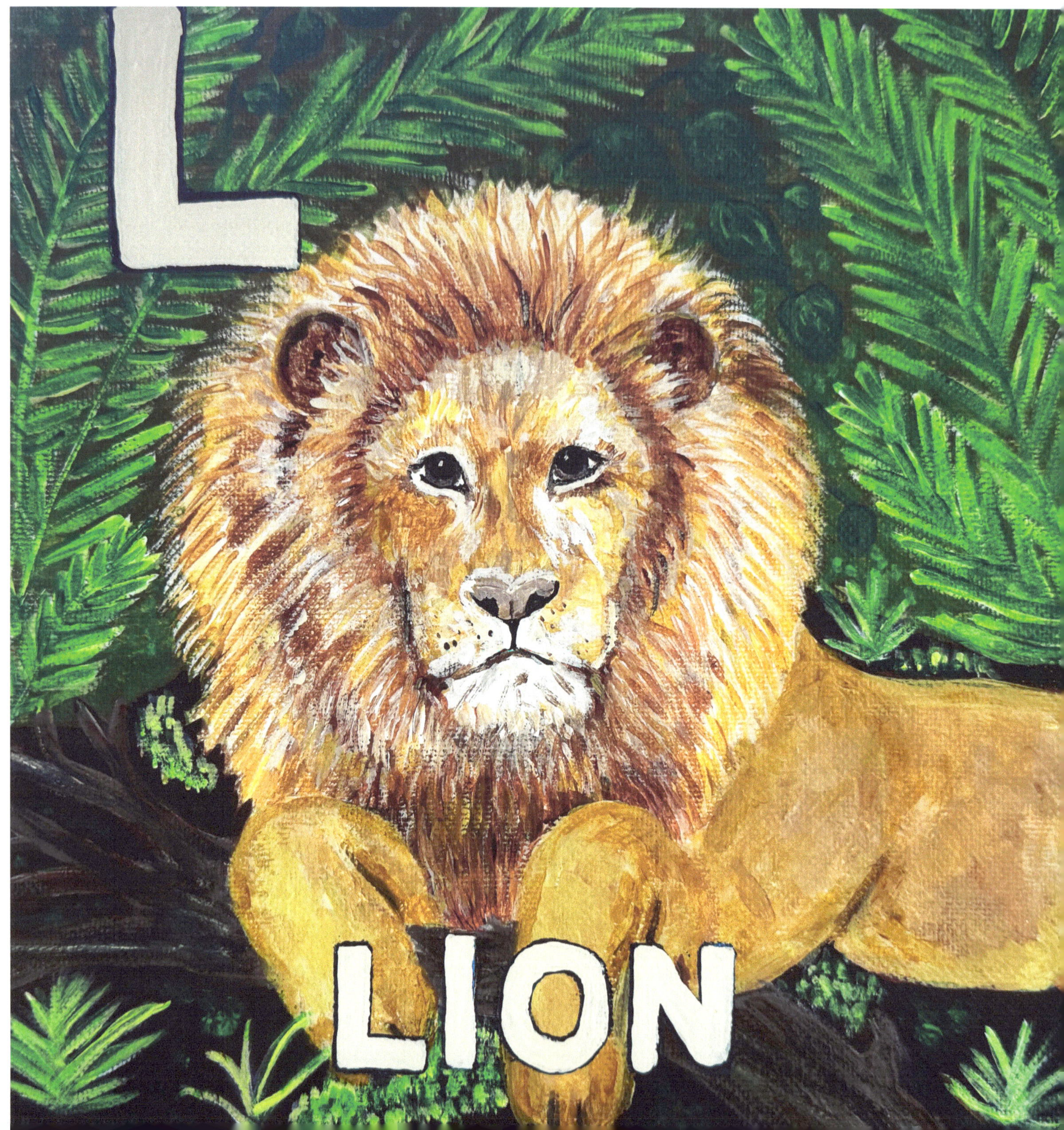

L
LION

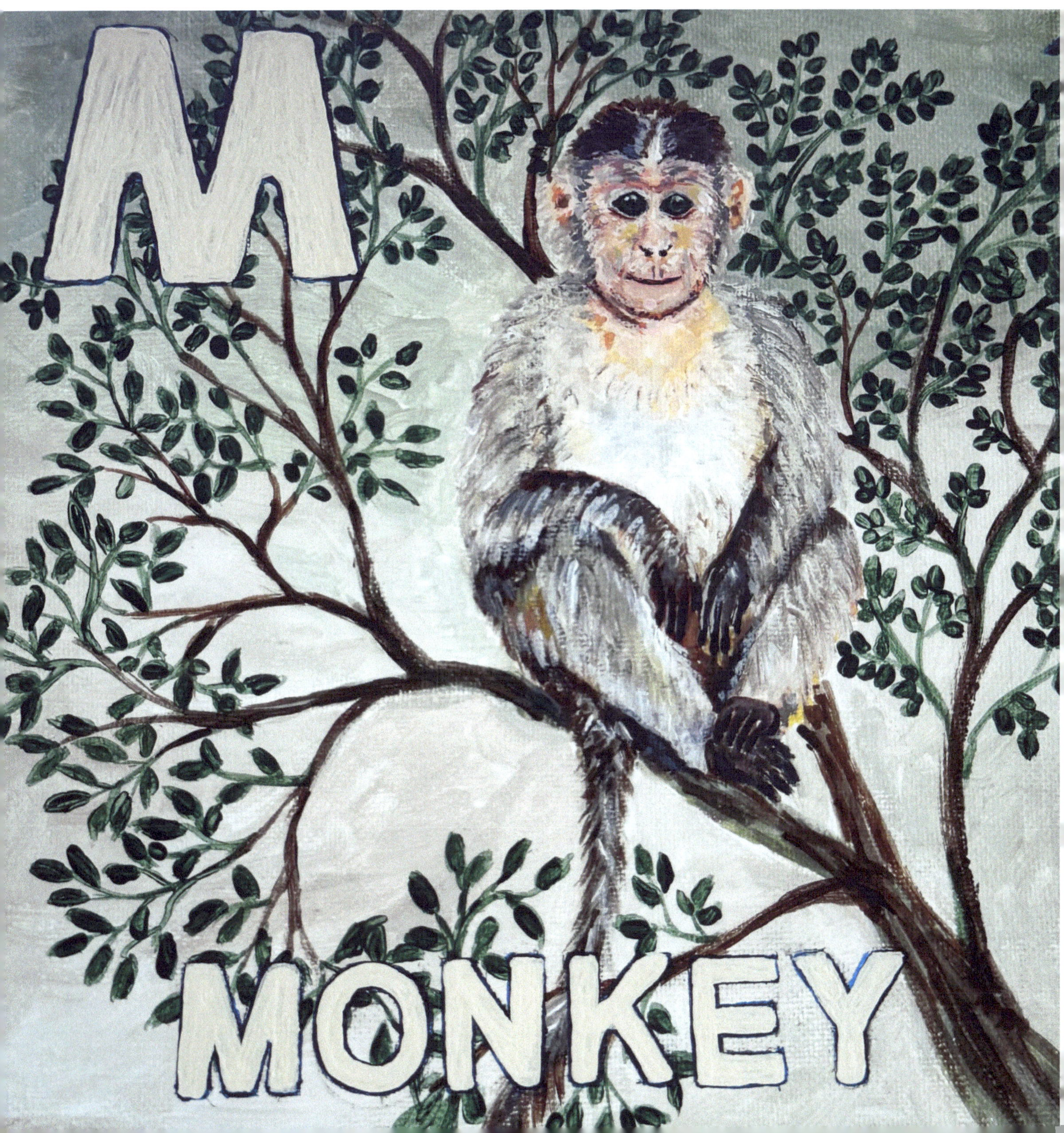
M
MONKEY

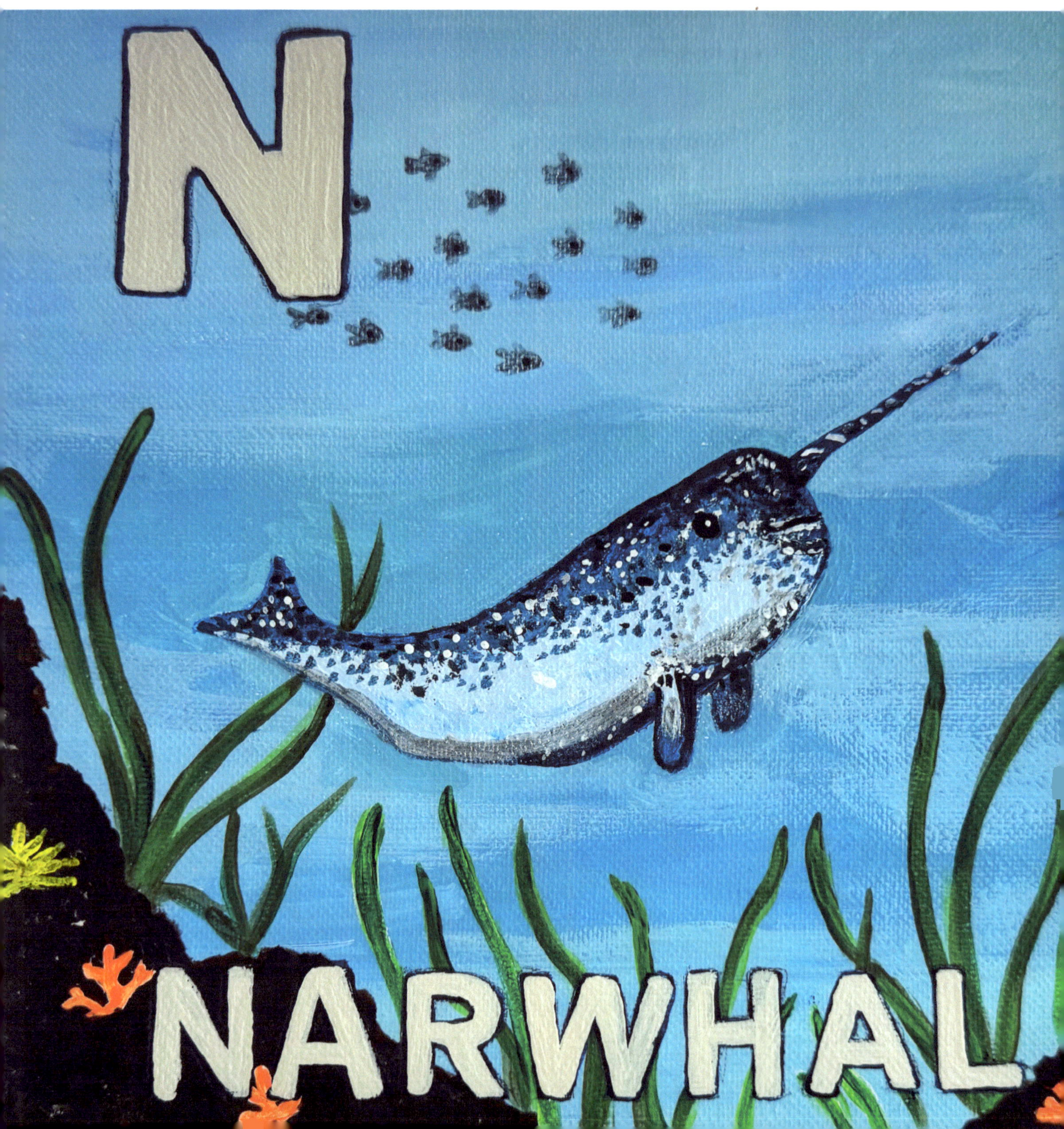

N
NARWHAL

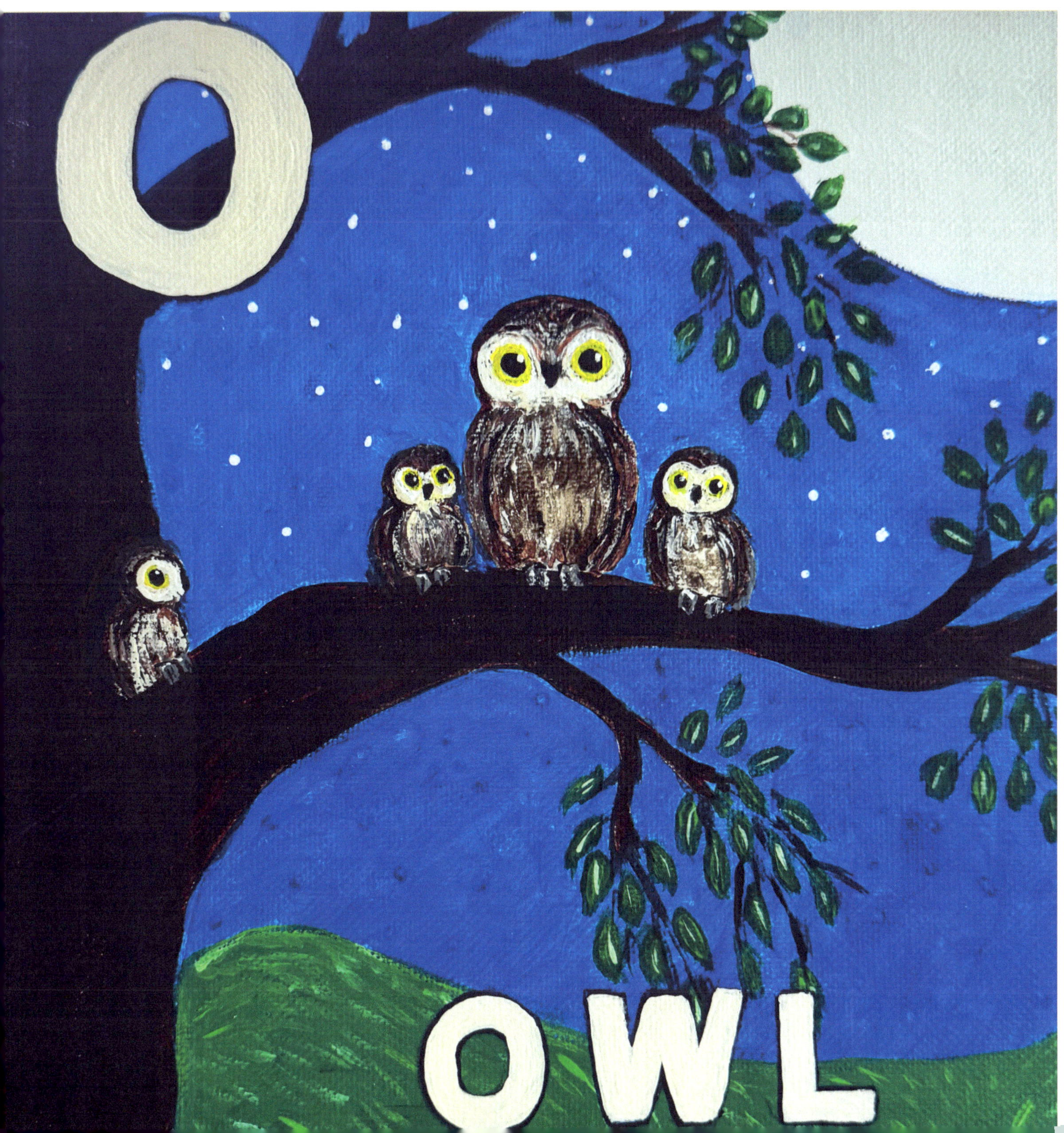

O
OWL

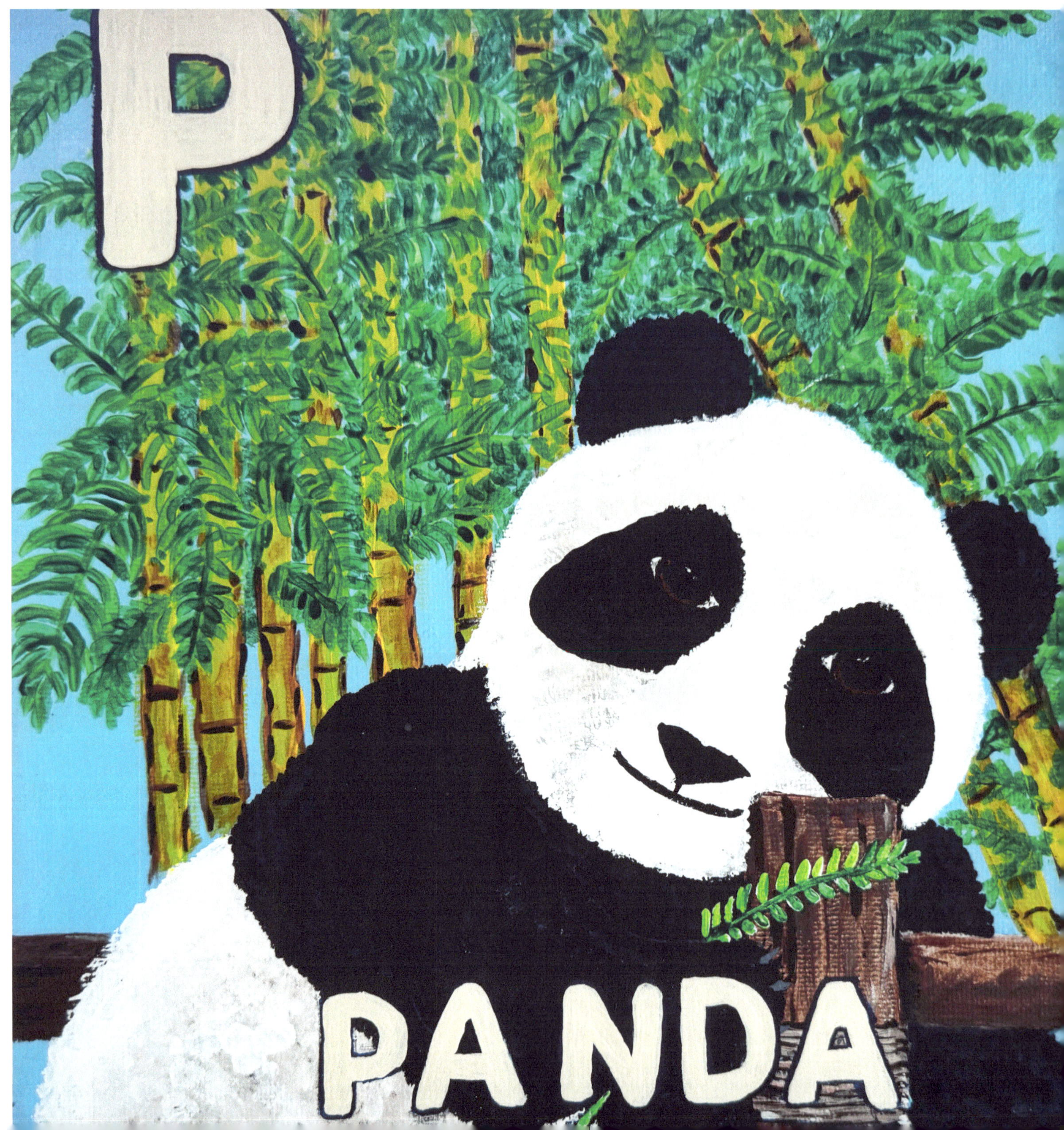

P
PANDA

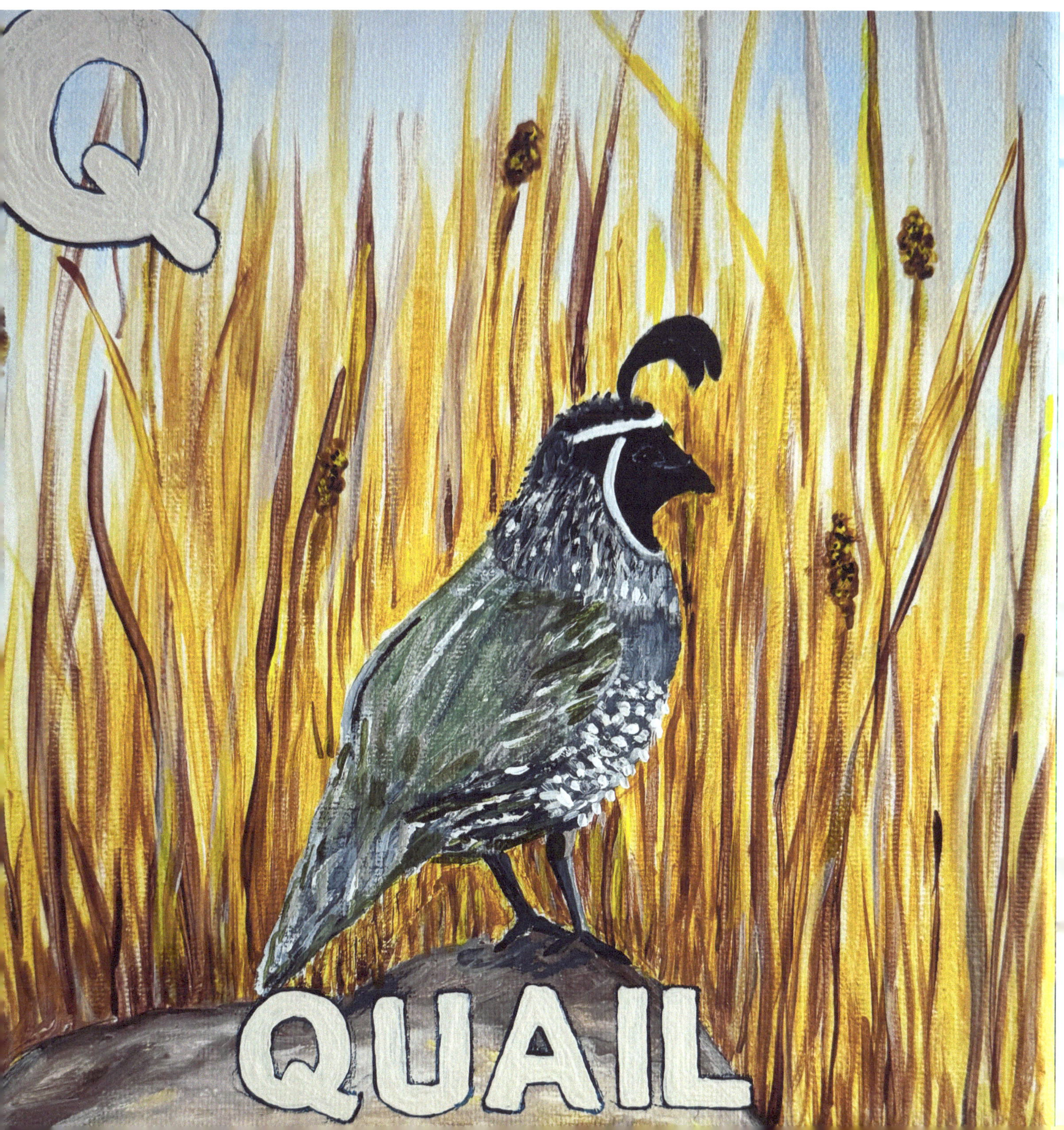

Q
QUAIL

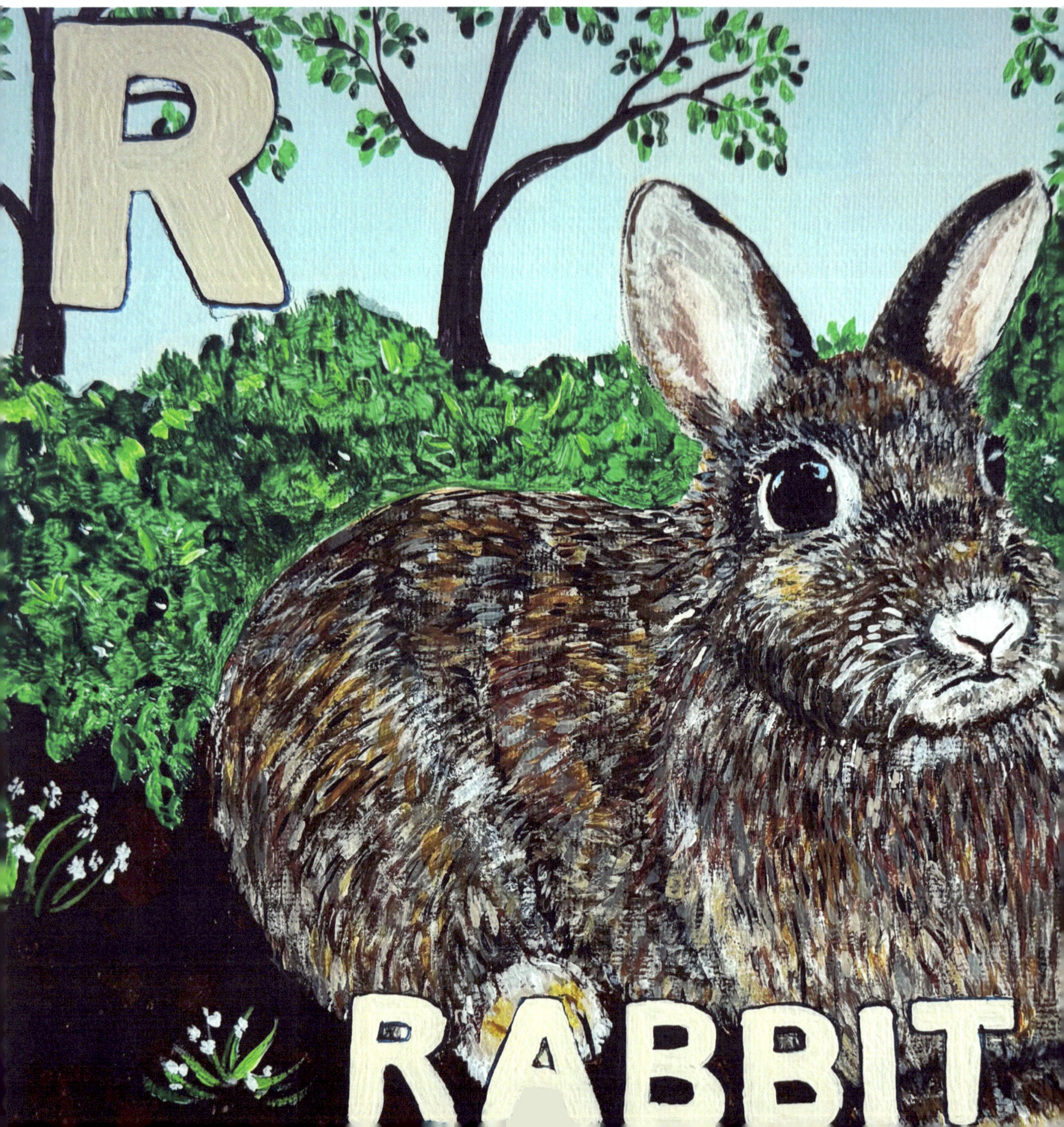

R
RABBIT

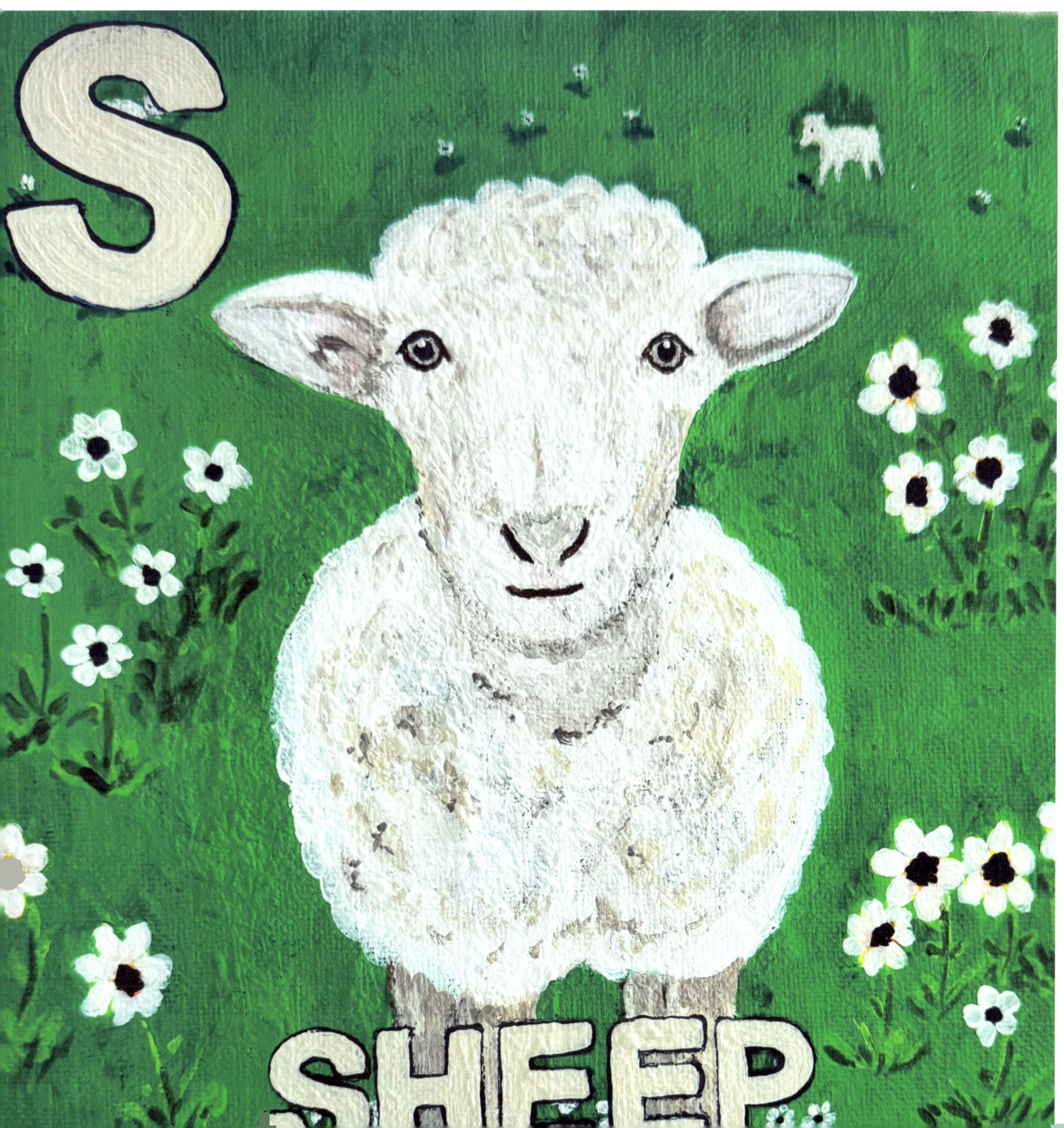

S
SHEEP

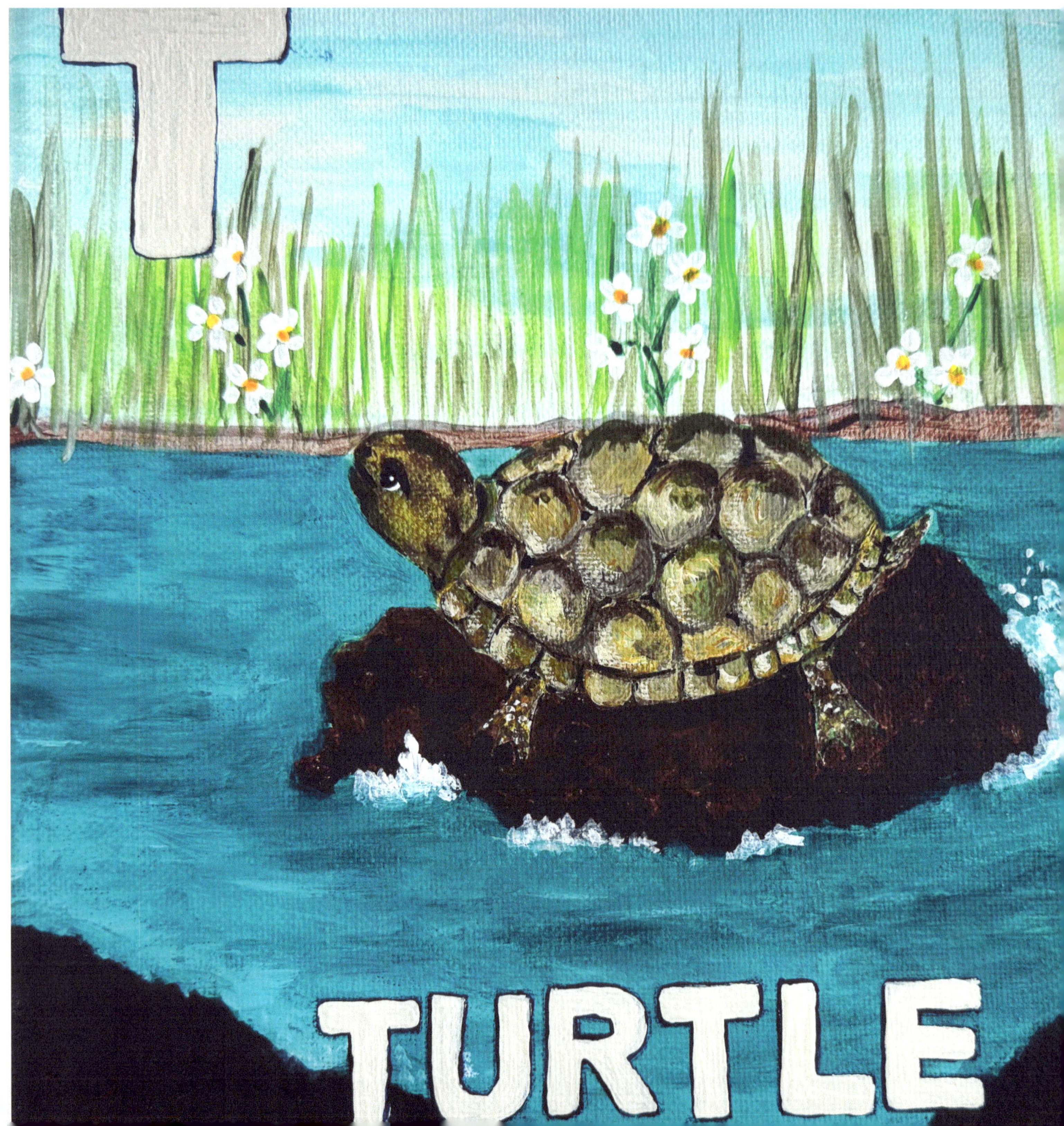

T
TURTLE

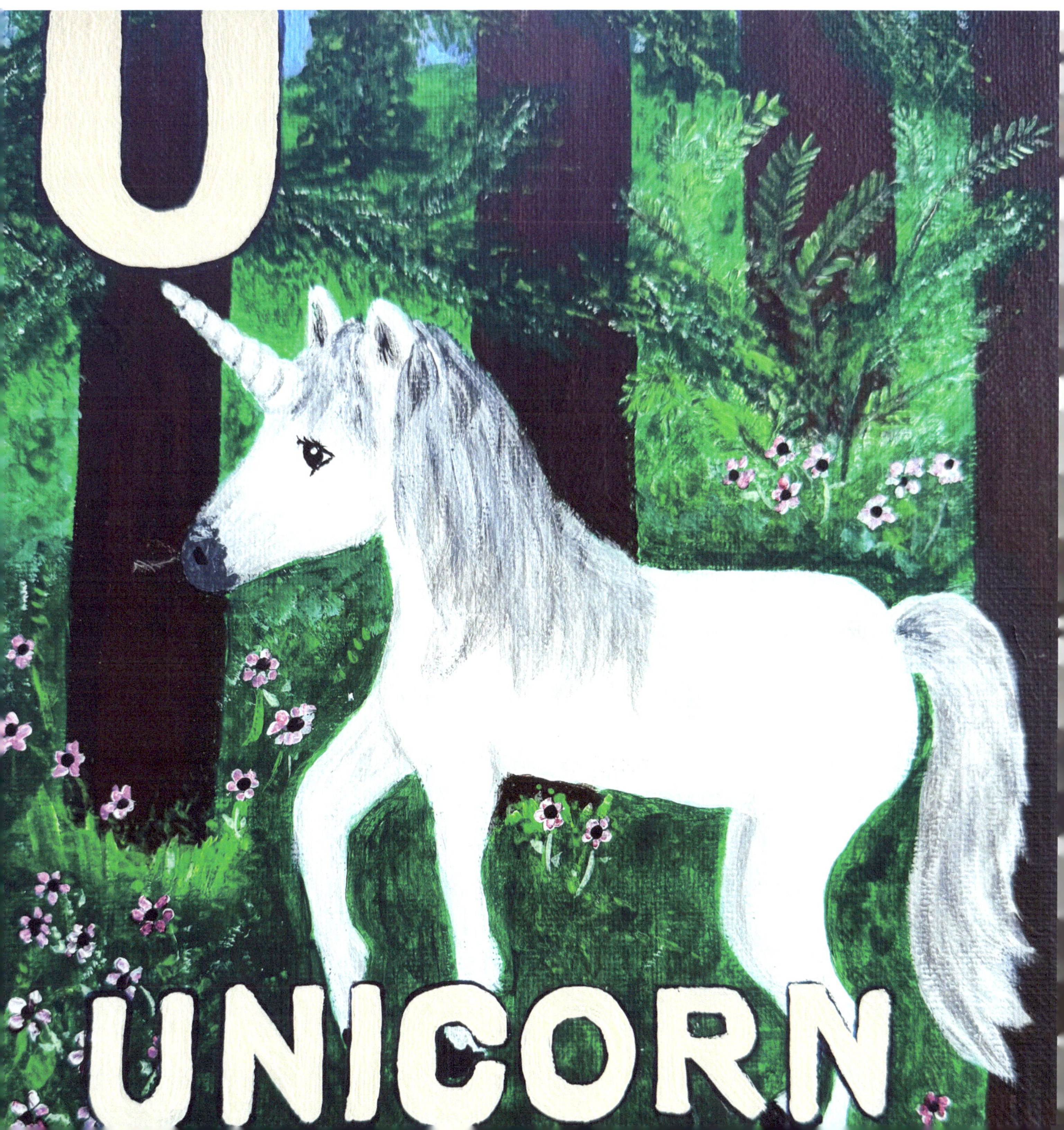
U
UNICORN

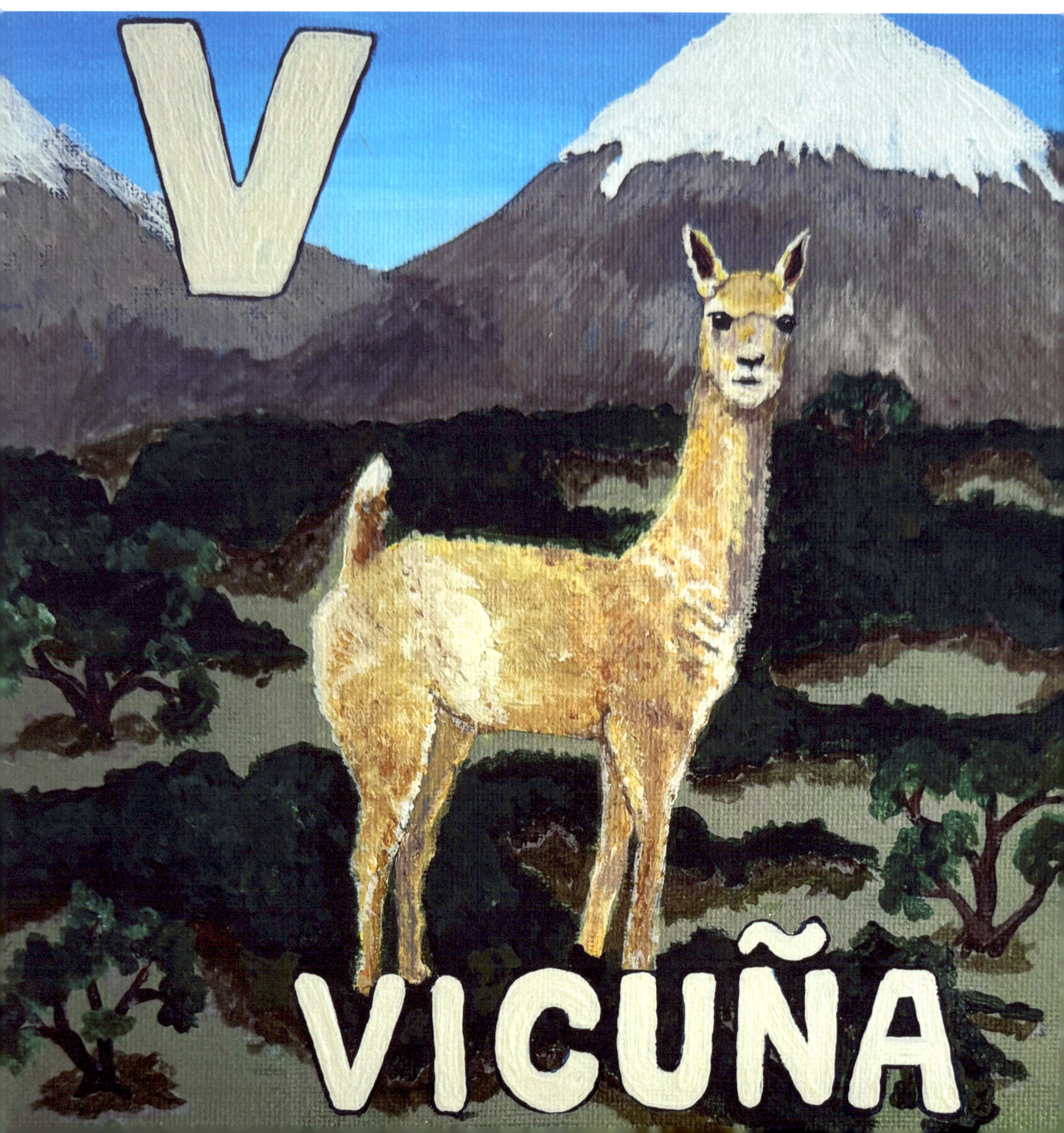

V
VICUÑA

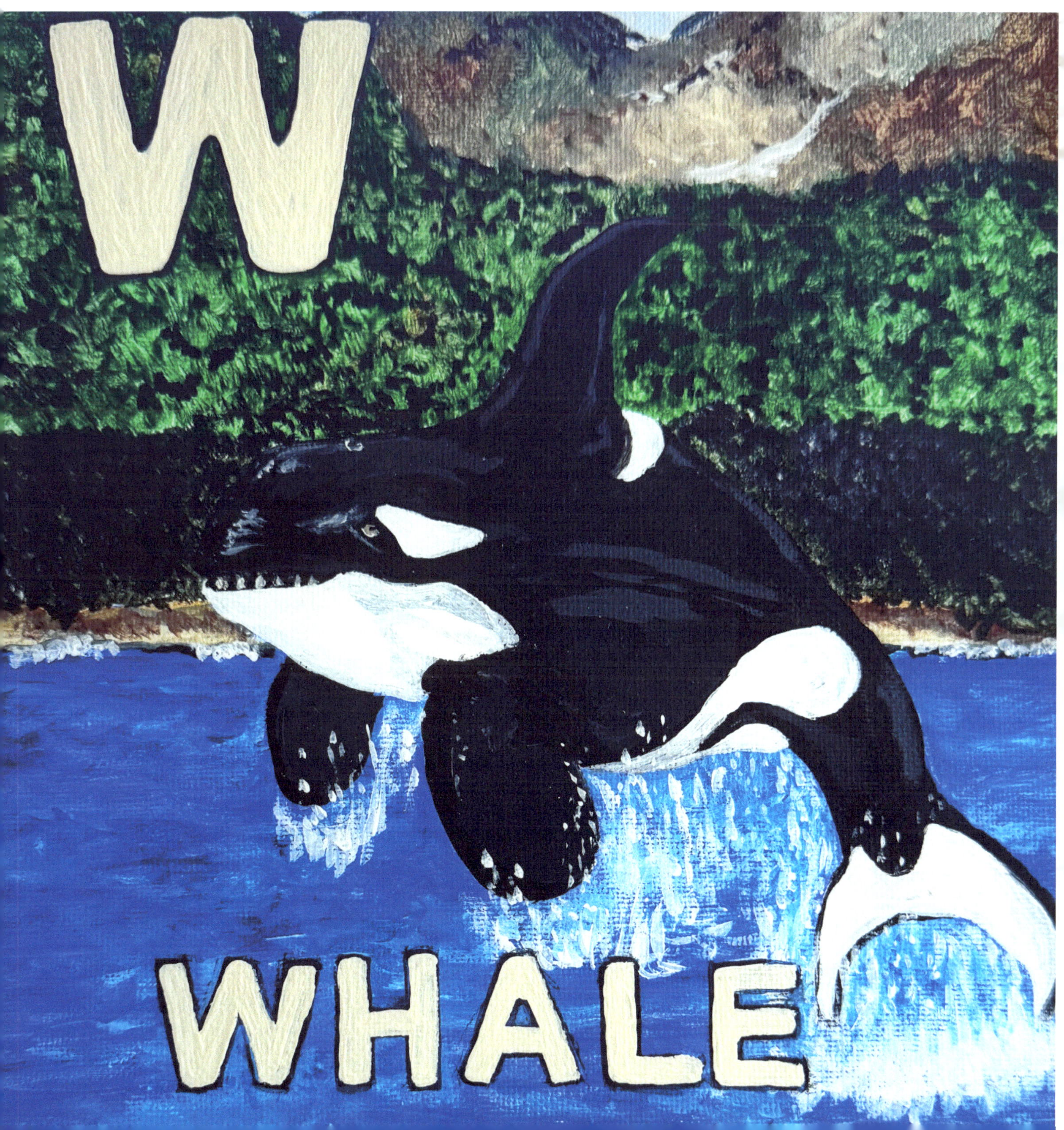

W
WHALE

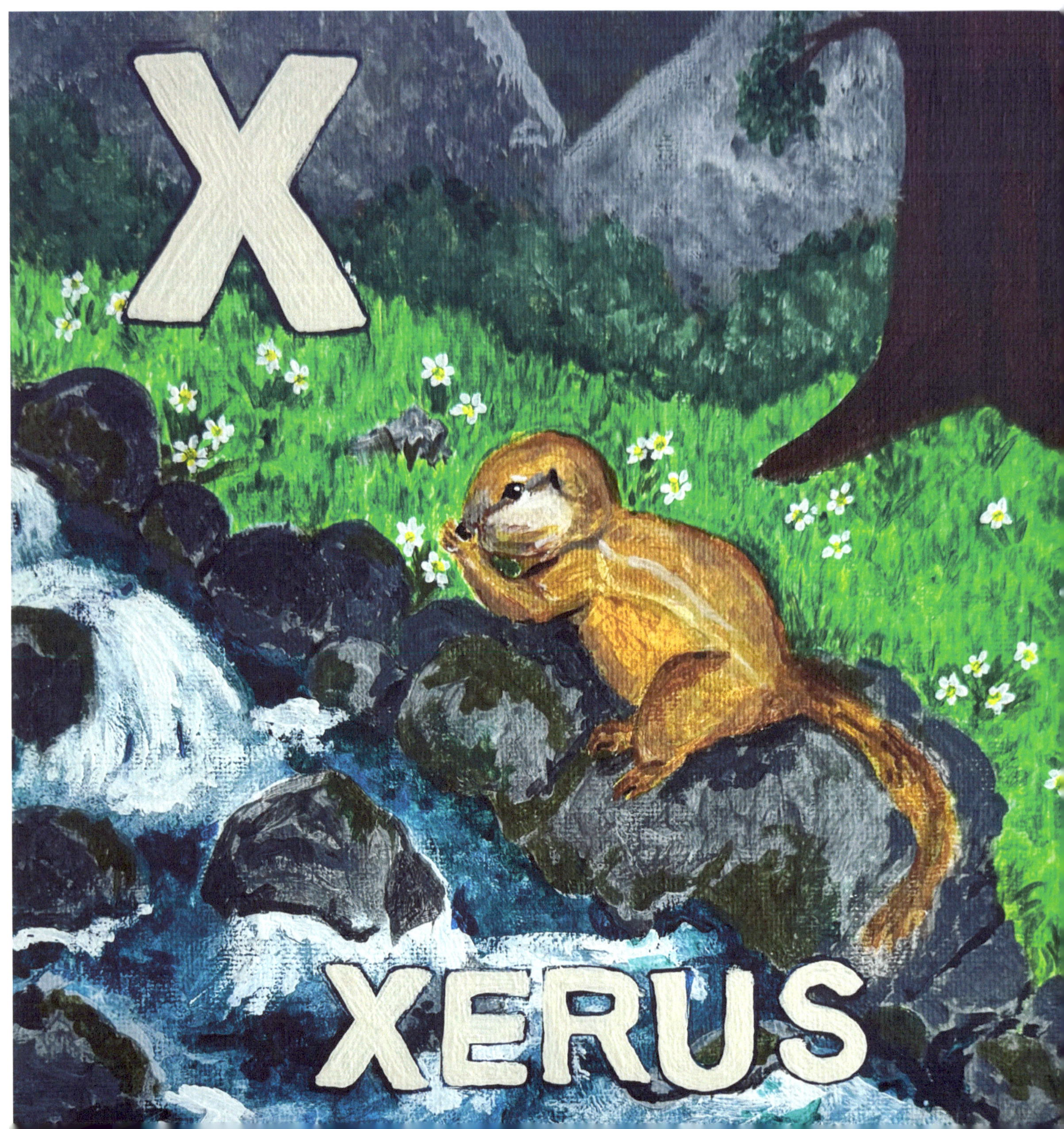
X
XERUS

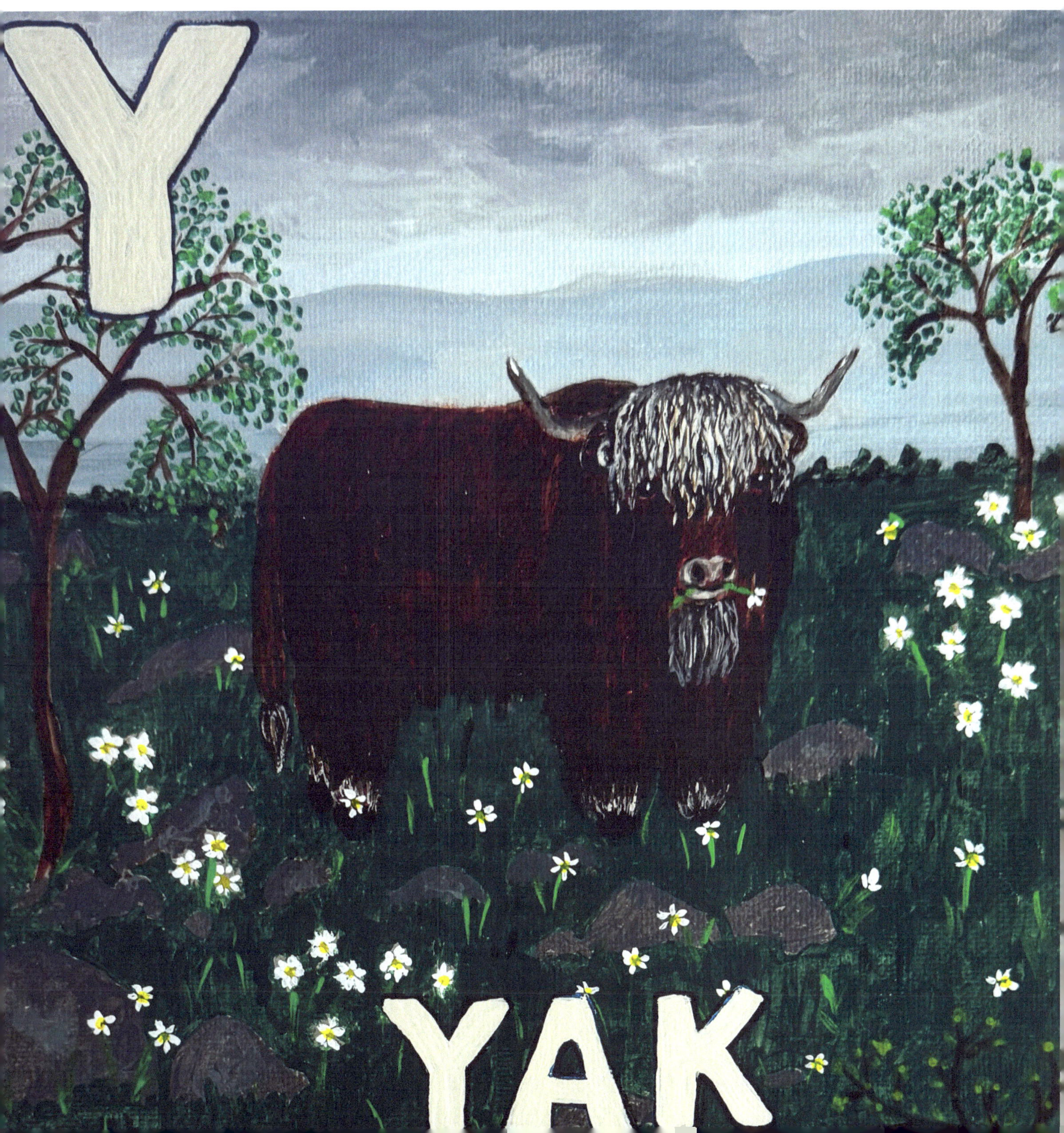

Y
YAK

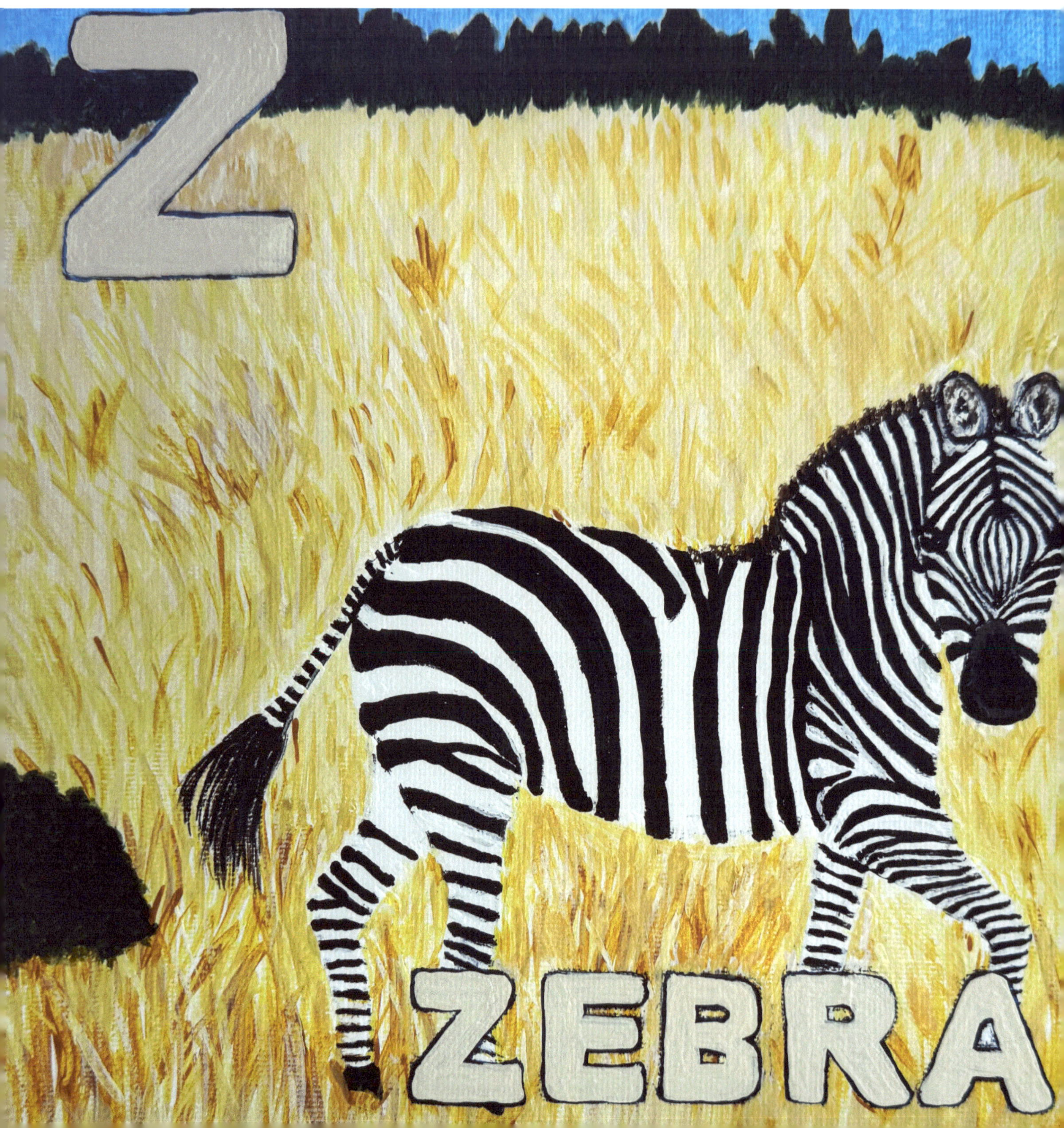

Z
ZEBRA

www.ingramcontent.com/pod-product-compliance
Lightning Source LLC
Chambersburg PA
CBHW042132030726
47599CB00002B/439